THE CHARCOAL COMPANION®
GRILLED
CHEESE
GRILLING BOOK

©2015 The Companion Group

Berkeley, California

800-521-0505

www.companion-group.com

INTRODUCTION

RECIPES

INTRODUCTION

If American culture – and even the global zeitgeist – is dominated by nostalgia, our food is no exception. The silliest fashions from the past are back in style, that terrible TV show from your childhood is getting a reboot, and the simplest comfort foods are experiencing their own renaissance. Mac 'n cheese, s'mores, burgers, and grilled cheese— of course!

Grilled cheese sandwiches were born during the Great Depression, and have been popular ever since, due to their simple ingredients and preparation. Like many foods they have been recently reinvented, and can be found in food trucks, trendy restaurants, as well as food blogs dedicated to this perfect, melty meal. So it would seem only natural to combine this classic American sandwich with America's favorite way to cook: on the grill!

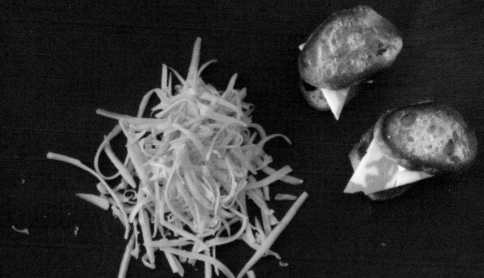

Outdoor cooking enthusiasts are using their charcoal or gas grills for more than just weekend cookouts, and grilling cheese sandwiches can become an easy, customizable meal for any day of the week. It's the perfect crowd pleaser for kids and adults alike! No need for greasy griddles in the kitchen; grillmasters can make cheese sandwiches either directly over an open flame, in a basket, or on a grid, using a variety of tools and methods.

The grilled cheese sandwich requires only three essential ingredients. Throughout this book, we have upgraded the classic sandwich with different variations of cheeses, breads, and butter. But why stop there when you're out at the grill? Why not throw in a few twists, like meats or grilled veggies – even fruit? Try wood smoking chips over the flames so that your sandwich will take on the rich, smoky flavors that only a barbecue can provide. Like everything else you can throw on a grill, the possibilities are endless. Enjoy experimenting, and give new meaning to the term "grilled cheese".

Now— It's time to put that grilled cheese on the grill!

THE BREAD

E ven though it was the development of mass-produced sliced bread that spurred the creation and popularity of the grilled cheese sandwich, you don't have to stick to just two boring loaf slices. Fresh bread is the best bread for anything, including grilled cheese! Artisanal bread bought from bakeries is meant for immediate consumption, and its freshness is reflected in its taste and texture. These breads often use very few ingredients (a good sign), avoiding preservatives and "filler ingredients" like high fructose corn syrup.

Also in this book, we experiment with different bread types. Beyond traditional loaves, there are buns, bagels, flatbreads, even croissants! Some of these breads have more unusual shapes and require a little extra prep. You may not need to butter the outside, or you may need a press to ensure the bread makes full contact with your grill. More dense breads might take longer to cook, while lighter, more delicate breads only need a light toasting. It can be a challenge to balance the time required to cook the bread and the time required to melt the cheese inside the sandwich; heavy breads that take a long time to crisp can result in cheese that's overcooked and dry. Be sure to follow our recommended cook times to get the perfect combination of crispy bread and gooey cheese!

TYPES OF CHEESES

[parmesan]

Soft Cheeses

Soft (but not fresh) cheeses, like blue cheese, often have lower moisture contents than their fresh counterparts. They also tend to ha more complex flavo

To better understand how cheese will melt when making a grilled cheese sandwich, we need to first take a look at the different types of cheeses. For our recipes, we carefully blended different cheeses based on volume versus potency of flavor, and made sure to select cheese that would cook well on the grill. Strong flavored cheeses were kept in lower proportion to more mild cheeses to balance the overall taste. When creating your own cheese combinations, try experimenting with two or three at a time, balancing strength and texture for the ultimate sandwich.

[marscapone]

Fresh Cheeses

Fresh cheeses aren't aged, and flavors tend to be more on the subtle side. The texture is almost always on the soft side, therefore taking very little time to melt. Also, moisture content is usually higher, due to the methods in which they're made, so you'll have to consider your oth ingredients when using this cheese in order to avoid soggy bread. Fresh cheeses should be gently warmed or heated until they're just starting to melt. Examples: Fresh Mozzarella, Marscapone, Ricotta, Chevre, and Crescenza.

6

...an fresh cheeses, due ... longer aging/ripening ...ocesses. Soft cheeses ...e similar to fresh when ...comes to melting, which ...akes them perfect for a ...lled cheese.
...amples: Brie, Blue ...eese, Camembert, ...aumes, Feta, and ...orgonzola.

[cheddar]

Semi-Hard Cheeses

These cheeses can be shredded or sliced due to the fair amount of moisture they contain. Neither hard nor soft, these cheeses are typically moderate to strong in flavor.
Examples: Cheddar, Colby, Monterey Jack, Gouda, Edam, & Gloucester.

...lue cheese]

Hard Cheeses

In most cases, hard cheeses are the oldest of the four categories. These cheeses are aged anywhere from 6-24 months (and sometimes even longer). Because of their density and the lack of moisture, they tend to melt best in a grilled cheese when they're shredded or grated into smaller pieces (as opposed to slicing them).
Examples: Beemster, Pecorino, Parmesan, Aged Gouda, Manchego and Wensleydale.

[fresh mozzarella]

[duck fat]

[olive oil]

[butter

[mayonnaise]

BUTTER & OTHER FATS

Spreading a fat-based ingredient on the outside of your bread is what gives it that crispy texture, as opposed to one that's dry and toasty. In effect, the thin layer of fat fries the surface of the bread when heat is applied. It also helps seal in moisture within the bread; this makes the bread pliable, not breakable. Of course, whether you use butter, oil, or something else on the outside of your bread depends on the kind of bread you're using. But if you're using a traditional sliced bread, you'll likely need to give it a few swipes of one of the following.

BUTTER

If the label says "You Can't Believe It's Not" what it's supposed to be, don't buy it! High quality, natural ingredients matter in all foods, and butter is no exception. When shopping for butter, look for keywords like "organic" and "grass-fed." When it comes to sandwiches, unsalted butter is best – after all, you're going to be adding other ingredients to the mix, and they might be salty enough on their own. Final tip: be sure to take the butter out of the fridge ahead of time so it's easy to spread!

OILS & OTHER FATS

Other everyday ingredients can be used to moisten and seal the outside of your sandwich; mayo and olive oil are both common in the kitchen. Others may require a bit of planning. Save the fat in the pan after cooking up some bacon (extra-convenient if you're already planning to use that bacon in your sandwich!). More esoteric fats, like duck fat, can be purchased in fine food stores. All of these fats have their own unique tastes, which may or may not suit your sandwich better than butter. Some of our recipes call for these different fats with this already in mind.

GRILLING TOOLS & COOKING METHODS

THE GRILLED CHEESE BASKET - Putting your sandwich in this basket gives you complete control to instantly move or flip your sandwich, simply by grabbing the handle. Preheat the basket with the grill for 5-7 minutes over direct flame, open it up and carefully load it with your sandwich(es). Close and lock the hinged lid and move the basket to indirect heat (to avoid any flare-ups). Once some of the butter has rendered, return the grid to direct medium-low flame and finish cooking your sandwich 4-6 minutes per side until crispy and cheese has melted.

THE GRILL PRESS - For those of you in search of a perfect sear every time, this will be your new favorite tool. Grill presses are handy when used in conjunction with a pre-heated base, like a grill grid, griddle, or pan. After putting your sandwich on the cooking surface, simply place the press on top and gently push down. The press will promote a nice, even, golden-brown surface by ensuring good contact between the bread and the cooking surface. Cook approximately 2-6 minutes per side, depending on the cooking surface you're using, until crispy and cheese has melted.

THE GRILLED CHEESE SPATULA - When using a pan, griddle, or grid to cook your grilled cheese on the grill, you'll need one more tool to help with the process – a good spatula. It's easy to think any old kitchen spatula would do, but in this case a spatula that's a little thinner and wider than your average type is preferable. This allows you to get underneath the sandwich easily, and with enough support to handle wide pieces of bread.

THE GRILL GRID - One discovery we made while making this cookbook is that grill grids do a great job searing grilled cheese sandwiches. The perforated surface of the grid allows smoke to penetrate through to the sandwich, adding that smoky bbq flavor we all love. Preheat the grid 8-12 minutes over medium flame. Once preheated, move the grid to indirect heat (to avoid any flare-ups) and place your sandwich on the grid. Once some of the butter has rendered, return the grid to direct flame and finish cooking your sandwich 4-6 minutes per side until crispy and cheese has melted.

CAST IRON PAN - Although it takes a little longer to preheat on the grill, cast iron is a great tool to use when cooking your grilled cheese. These pans retain heat well and produce a nice crispy surface when frying up the bread. Cast iron pans work even better when paired with a grill press. This is especially true for cast iron pans that have ridges on the bottom. To make a grilled cheese on cast iron, simply preheat the pan over medium flame for 6-8 minutes. Once the pan is hot, place your sandwich inside and cook 2-3 minutes per side until crispy.

THE GRIDDLE - Breakfast griddles for the grill also make a great option for cooking grilled cheese sandwiches. Usually, griddles are big enough to hold 3 or 4 sandwiches, which comes in handy for feeding more than two people. Some grills even have a dedicated griddle built into the side for cooking breakfast foods or other items. These same griddles also work great for sizzling up some grilled cheese gooeyness.

gouda inside & out

GOUDA, SWISS & PARMESAN

Sometimes you need to look at things from a new perspective. In this case, what about putting cheese on the OUTSIDE of the sandwich? By encrusting the bread with a layer of parmesan, you get the ultimate crunchy exterior. The cheese fries up crispy and delicious, with a tang tempered by the more mellow cheese inside.

2 slices white bread

2 slices swiss cheese

½ cup gouda, shredded

2 Tbsp. parmesan, shredded

2 tsp. quality butter

Method:

Preheat your tools and grill according to the cooking methods on page 10-11. Butter the top side of each slice of bread. Place half the parmesan cheese on one slice of bread (directly on the butter), and repeat with the other slice of bread.

Take one slice of bread and place onto the non-stick cooking surface, cheese/butter side down. Add two slices of swiss and shredded gouda then place remaining slice of bread on top, cheese/butter side up. Cook approximately 4-6 minutes per side until cheese inside has melted and outside is crisp.

COOKING TIP: For this sandwich it's a good idea to use a non-stick cooking surface, so the cheese doesn't stick.

truffle shuffle

PORTOBELLO, FONTINA & TRUFFLED CHEDDAR

E arthy Portobello mushrooms are grilled to perfection and accented by a rich, flavorful truffled pecorino cheese. If you can't find truffled pecorino in your area, pick up a small bottle of truffle oil and drizzle it on top of the cheese before you close up the sandwich.

2 slices sourdough bread

1 small portobello mushroom

¼ cup fontina cheese, shredded

2 Tbsp. truffled cheddar or pecorino cheese, shredded

2 tsp. quality butter

Method:

Begin by cleaning any excess dirt from your mushroom. Remove stem and brush mushroom with olive oil. Grill 5-6 minutes per side over medium high heat until cooked through. Let cool and slice mushroom into ¼" strips.

Preheat your tools and grill according to the cooking methods on page 10-11. Butter the top side of each slice of bread.

Take one slice in your hand (butter side down) and add all of the cheese. Place mushrooms onto the cheese and top with the other slice of buttered bread. Transfer to the grilled cheese basket or grid and grill 4-6 minutes per side until bread is toasted and cheese has melted.

BEVERAGE TIP: If you'd really like to go all out, pair this sandwich with a nice Pinot Noir.

some like it rye

RYE, FONTINA MIX, WITH CREAMY TOMATO SOUP

Making a grilled cheese cookbook without including tomato soup would be a crime against food! So here it is: our take on the classic grilled cheese sandwich with tomato soup. This recipe is the perfect warm, cozy lunch for crisp, cold days; the hearty rye bread with rich cheese combo is ideal for cutting into small slices to dip into your creamy tomato soup.

Sandwich:

2 slices rye bread

1 slice provolone

¼ cup fontina, shredded

1 tsp. parmesan reggiano

2 tsp. quality butter

Soup:

(1) 12 oz. can organic fire roasted tomatoes

¼ to ½ cup whipping cream

¼ yellow onion, small dice

1 tsp. salt

1 tsp. olive oil

Method:

In a medium sized pot, sauté diced onion until translucent. Add tomatoes and cream and simmer 20 minutes on low heat until flavors combine. Purée mixture with an immersion blender until smooth. If desired, pass through a thin mesh sieve or strainer for a silky smooth consistency.

Preheat your tools and grill according to the cooking methods on page 10-11. Butter the top side of each slice of bread. Take one slice in your hand (butter side down) and add the provolone, fontina, and parmesan.

Transfer to the preheated grill and cook 4-6 minutes per side until bread is toasted and cheese has melted. Serve alongside tomato soup.

BEVERAGE TIP: This sandwich pairs best with Belgian style ales such as Chimay or Duvel.

SAFFRON BUTTER & SERRANO HAM

Spain is home to a number of unique, region-specific culinary staples. This sandwich features three ingredients often found in true Spanish cuisine: Manchego cheese, Jamón Serrano, and saffron. If you're feeling extra gourmet, replace the Serrano ham with Iberco and prepare to be amazed.

¼ gram saffron, minced

2 tsp. quality butter

¼ cup whole milk mozzarella, shredded

2 Tbsp.. Manchego cheese

2 slices Serrano (or Iberco) ham

2 slices white bread

Method:

Preheat your tools and grill according to the cooking methods on page 10-11. Soften butter by microwaving 10-12 seconds. Add minced saffron and butter together in a small bowl and whip with a small whisk to combine. Spread each piece of bread with half the saffron butter. Take one slice in your hand (fat side down) and add one slice of ham. Place half the grated Manchego and mozzarella on top of ham.

Add the second piece of ham and remaining cheese and top with remaining slice of bread. Transfer to preheated grill and cook 4-6 minutes per side until bread is crispy and cheese has melted.

BEVERAGE TIP: Sangria is a great beverage to pair with this sandwich and its Spanish styling.

the new yorke

CREAM CHEESE & GORGONZOLA ON A BAGEL

This tasty sandwich is the perfect way to kick your breakfast into overdrive. Say goodbye to your plain old bagel 'n schmear and say hello to a wonderfully rich cream cheese spiked with gorgonzola. Fresh chives perfectly complement both types cheeses as well as the onion bagel.

1 onion bagel

3 Tbsp. cream cheese

2 tsp. gorgonzola cheese

1 Tbsp. chopped chives

2 tsp. quality butter

Method:

Allow both cheeses to soften at room temperature for 20-30 minutes before preparing sandwich. Cut bagel in half and spread butter on the inside of each piece. Once both cheeses have softened add them to a small bowl with half of the chives. Mix ingredients thoroughly in a bowl by using small whisk or spatula. Preheat your tools and grill according to the cooking methods on page 10-11.

Grill buttered bagel slices until golden and crispy, approximately 4-6 minutes.

Spread half cheese/onion mixture across the inside of both bagel pieces and put the two sides together.

BEVERAGE TIP: This sandwich makes a great way to start the day when paired with a hot cup of dark roast coffee.

the bpt

BRIE, PANCETTA, & HEIRLOOM TOMATO RELISH

The BLT has to be one of the most classic, simple and tastiest sandwiches around. Taking a few cues from this deli favorite, we've put a cheesed up spin on it with mozzarella and an amazing triple-cream Black Label Cambozola. Bacon has been upgraded to pancetta, while the standard sliced tomatoes have been replaced with a delicious, seasonal heirloom tomato relish.

Sandwich:

2 oz. Black Label Cambozola*

¼ cup shredded mozzarella

3 thin slices (cooked) pancetta

2 slices rustic sourdough

2 tsp. quality butter

Relish:

1 small heirloom tomato

1 small clove garlic

1 tsp. extra virgin olive oil

Pinch of pepper

¼ tsp. red wine vinegar

Method:

To prepare relish, chop tomato and garlic finely, add remaining relish ingredients and mix to combine. Render thinly sliced (or chopped) pancetta in a cast iron pan over low heat until crispy

Preheat your tools and grill according to the cooking methods on page 10-11. Butter the top side of each slice of bread. Take one slice in your hand (butter side down) and add the mozzarella, pancetta and cambozola. Add 2 tsp. of relish over the top of the cheese and top with the other slice of buttered bread. Transfer to the preheated grill and cook 4-6 minutes per side until bread is toasted and cheese has melted.

*If you can't find cambozola at your local store, feel free to substitute your choice of blue-brie instead.

BEVERAGE TIP: A luscious glass of Pinot Bianco goes well with the hearty flavors of this fresh tomato relish.

the trifecta

CHEDDAR, JALAPEÑOS, BACON & PRETZEL BUN

The trifecta, the holy trinity, or the three musketeers... whatever you'd like to call them, this combination of cheddar, bacon, and jalapeños is sent over the top on a deliciously chewy pretzel bun. Toasted to perfection, this sandwich isn't your average grilled cheese; it's all your favorite ingredients sandwiched between two pieces of bread.

¼ cup shredded mild cheddar

2 Tbsp. shredded sharp cheddar

3 strips thick cut bacon

1 small jalapeño pepper*

1 pretzel bun

Method:

Preheat a cast iron pan over medium flame 20-30 seconds until hot. Add bacon and cook 4-6 minutes per side until crispy, remove from pan and allow to cool. Cut bacon into ¼" pieces. Slice the jalapeño thinly and sauté for 45 seconds to 1 minute in the rendered bacon fat. Remove from pan and set aside.

Preheat your tools and grill according to the cooking methods on page 10-11. Cut pretzel bun in half and set aside.

Take the sliced pretzel bun and add the cheddar, jalapeños and bacon.

Top with the other slice of bread and transfer to the grill. Grill 3-4 minutes per side until bread is toasted and cheese has melted.

*If you desire a less spicy sandwich, consider removing the seeds and pith from the jalapeño.

BEVERAGE TIP:
Try this sandwich with
a tasty craft IPA such as
Lagunitas or Racer 5.

sweet dubliner

DUBLINER CHEDDAR, SWISS, WILD HONEY & PEAR

The best part of a well-aged cheddar cheese is the tiny little salt crystals that form during the aging process called tyrosine. For most people, it's a welcome interruption from the smooth, creamy texture of the cheese. You can even feel the crunch when you bite into a nutty, deliciously sharp piece of well-made cheese. Paired with wild honey and Asian pear, the cheddar really shines in this recipe. For the best results, be sure you're using only the ripest of pears.

2 slices walnut-raisin bread

1 slice swiss cheese

¼ cup cheddar, Kerrigold Dubliner brand

½ tsp. wild honey

2 tsp. quality butter

1 Hosui (Asian) pear

Method:

Preheat your tools and grill according to the cooking methods on page 10-11. Slice pear into thin slices. Butter the top side of each slice of bread. Take one slice in your hand (butter side down) and add the cheddar and pears, drizzling honey over the top to finish.

Top with the other slice of buttered bread. Transfer to the preheated grill and cook 4-6 minutes per side until bread is toasted and cheese has melted.

BEVERAGE TIP: A dry mead (honey) wine matches well with the flavors and can contrast the sweetness of this dish.

spicy muenster

SPICY MAYO, MUENSTER & SERRANO CHILI

While traditional grilled cheese sandwiches are made with butter on the outside, they don't have to be. We're giving butter a rest and instead creating a spicy mayo to slather on our sourdough. Using mayo also allows us to further customize the sandwich by adding in some spice! The flavorful exterior of the sandwich echoes its potent filling.

1 tsp. Sriracha

2 tsp. organic mayonnaise

2 slices muenster cheese

¼ tsp. smoked paprika

1 tsp. roasted red bell pepper, diced

1 tsp. serrano chili, minced

2 slices sourdough bread

Method:

Preheat your tools and grill according to the cooking methods on page 10-11. In a small bowl, combine mayo with Sriracha and mix thoroughly. Spread the top side of each slice of bread with half the mayo/ Sriracha mixture. Take one slice in your hand (fat side down) and add all the sliced cheese. Place bell peppers and serrano chilis on top of cheese and sprinkle with smoked paprika.

Add second slice of bread and transfer to grill. Cook 4-6 minutes per side until bread is crispy and cheese has melted.

COOKING TIP: For a less spicy sandwich, replace Sriracha with additional smoked paprika. Serrano chilis can also be removed.

grilled gouda-ness

CARAMELIZED ONIONS, GOUDA, & EMMENTAHLER

Inspired by a delicious, mouth-watering pizza with similar ingredients, this grilled cheese is packed with flavor. Sweet caramelized onions meld wonderfully with the nuttiness of Emmentahler cheese. Gouda brings a creamy infill with a slight tanginess at the end for a well-rounded and highly addictive flavor profile.

For caramelized onions:

1 tsp. extra virgin olive oil

1 yellow onion

Sandwich:

¼ cup shredded double cream gouda cheese

1 slice emmentahler cheese

2 slices wheat bread

2 tsp. quality butter

Method:

Begin by removing the top and bottom of the onion. Slice the onion lengthwise and remove the skin. Once onion is halved, cut into ¼" half-moon shaped pieces. In a large sauté pan, heat olive oil over medium flame until hot. Add onions to the pan and cook 20-30 minutes, stirring occasionally, until dark and caramelized. Meanwhile, preheat your tools and grill according to the cooking methods on page 10-11.

When onions are finished, transfer to a plate or baking sheet and set aside. Butter the top side of each slice of bread. Take one slice in your hand (butter side down) and add all of the cheese. Add 2 Tbsp. of caramelized onions, top with the other slice of buttered bread, and transfer to the grilled cheese basket. Grill 4-6 minutes per side until bread is toasted and cheese has melted.

COOKING TIP: For even more smoky, earthy flavor notes try grilling your onions using a grill wok or grid.

the blue box special

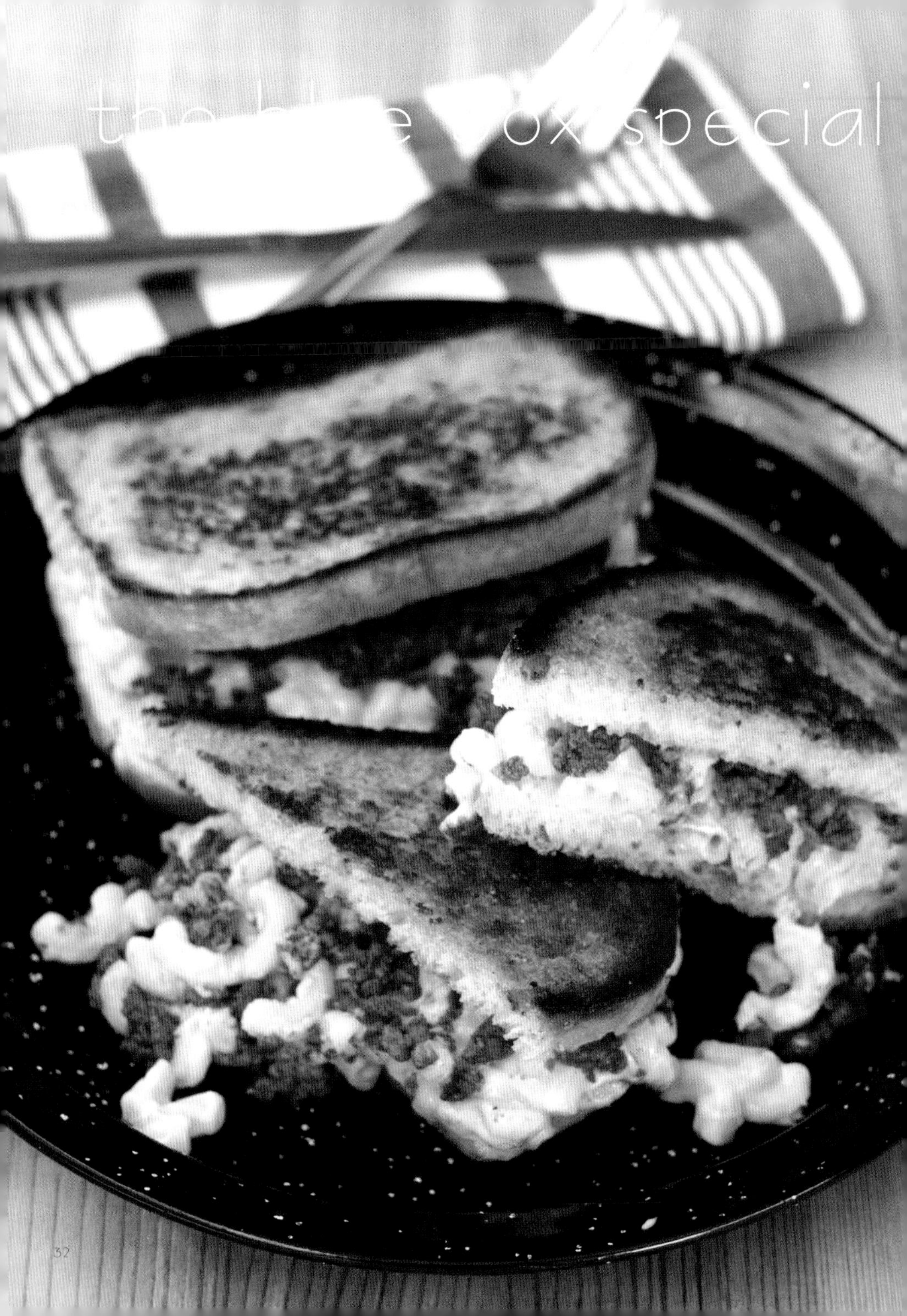

MAC 'N CHEESE & CHORIZO

What's the OTHER quintessentially American cheese-based dish? Mac and cheese! Mac n' cheese, like the grilled cheese sandwich, is also experiencing a resurgence of popularity and experimentation. We're thinking outside of the (blue cardboard) box and putting the cheesy pasta between two slices of bread. Add in some chorizo for a little kick and protein to this creamy, carb-loaded sandwich.

Pasta:

2 oz. taleggio cheese

2 oz. sharp cheddar cheese

2 oz. gouda cheese

2 oz. mozzarella cheese

1 cup elbow macaroni

¼ cup cream

2 tsp. arrowroot

Sandwich:

2 slices sourdough

2 Tbsp. cooked chorizo

2 tsp. quality butter

Method:

In a medium sized pot, boil 1½ quarts water. Once water is boiling, add pasta and cook 6-7 minutes until al dente (still has a bit of firmness). Drain water from pasta and place a few cups of ice on top, running water over the pasta to stop the cooking process. Combine arrowroot with 1 tsp. of cream and mix until dissolved. Bring remaining cream to a simmer using medium pot. Slowly incorporate arrowroot/cream mixture while stirring. Once arrowroot is fully incorporated, add cheeses slowly, one by one until completely dissolved. Continue stirring to avoid scorching. Once mixture has thickened, add cooked macaroni back into the cream/cheese mixture, stir thoroughly to combine and remove from heat. Allow mixture to cool slightly. Butter the outside of each slice of bread and place finished macaroni inside with the chorizo.

Preheat your tools and grill according to the cooking methods on page 10-11. Transfer your sandwich to the grill and cook 4-6 minutes per side until bread is toasted.

COOKING TIP: If you have an aversion to chorizo don't fret. Bacon makes a great replacement for a milder, familiar flavor combination.

HALLOUMI, TZATZIKI & TOAST

There are few cheeses that can actually be put directly on the grill, and Halloumi, with its high melting point, is one of them. Halloumi is a popular Mediterranean cheese that originated on the island country of Cyprus. It's often fried and then served in a number of different ways. In this recipe, the Halloumi is grilled until crispy and served on an open-face sandwich with a tangy tzatziki.

Method:

Sandwich:

¼ lb. Halloumi cheese

1 piece flat bread

Small handful mixed greens

Tzatziki:

6 oz. plain yogurt

1 tsp. lemon juice

2 Tbsp. cucumber, small dice

1 tsp. dill, minced

Cut Halloumi into two pieces approximately ¼" thick. Preheat your tools and grill according to the cooking methods on page 10-11. Brush each side of the cheese with olive oil and place on the hot grill, grilling 1-2 minutes per side. Meanwhile, place the flatbread over medium heat and grill 1-2 minutes per side. Place grilled cheese onto warm flat bread and top with Tzatziki and mixed greens.

COOKING TIP: When grilling the cheese, be sure of two things: your grill is really hot, and properly oiled. This way the cheese will sear nicely, without sticking to the grate.

morning companion

BACON & EGG

M̲ake any meal the most important of the day by having breakfast anytime! This sandwich is filled your morning classics: bacon and eggs. This sandwich is prepared open-faced at first and assembled with the cooked bacon and soft-boiled egg to finish. When the top slice of bread is placed on the sandwich, press down gently but firmly to drench all the ingredients in warm, delicious egg yolk. Serve with seasonal fresh fruit for a complete breakfast or brunch experience.

1 small organic egg

3 strips thick cut bacon

2 tsp. bacon fat

1 tsp. parmesan

¼ cup gruyère cheese, shredded

¼ cup cheddar cheese, shredded

2 slices sourdough bread

Method:

Prepare bacon by placing strips into a cold cast iron pan. Set the pan to medium low-flame and cook bacon, flipping every 2-3 minutes until crispy. Remove bacon from pan and set aside. Reserve the bacon fat by placing it into a small container to chill in the freezer for 15 minutes. Meanwhile, start a pot of boiling water. When water reaches a boil turn down to a simmer, then place the egg into the pot. Simmer 5-6 minutes, remove from pot, and run under cold tap water. Once cooled, gently crack and remove the shell.

Preheat your tools and grill according to the cooking methods on page 10-11. Once the bacon fat becomes spreadable, spread it onto the bread. Place one slice gruyère on each piece of bread and grill with the fat side down until the cheese melts. Remove bread slices from the grill, top with bacon and peeled egg. Place the other piece of bread on top and gently press down onto the egg until it breaks and the yolk runs all over the sandwich.

COOKING TIP: Serve with seasonal fresh fruit for a complete breakfast or brunch experience.

GRILLED CHEESE FUN FACTS

• During the Great Depression an open-faced sandwich called the "cheese dream" was popular. Cheese Dream, a warm slice of bread with melted cheese on top, was a direct descendent of the British "cheese on toast." Around the same time, the bread slicer and processed cheese were also invented. Eventually someone got the bright idea to add a second slice of bread and the grilled cheese sandwich was born.

• One of the most expensive grilled cheeses ever recorded cost $168. The sandwich had cheddar with white truffles, 100-year-old balsamic vinegar and slices of quail egg, black tomato, apple and fresh figs, all served on sourdough bread sprinkled with gold dust.

• In 2004, online casino GoldenPalace.com made an interesting purchase by paying $28,000 for a half-eaten grilled cheese sandwich with what looks like the Virgin Mary in the burn pattern. A Florida woman had kept the sandwich intact for a decade, before eventually selling it on eBay.

NATIONAL
Grilled Cheese
DAY
APRIL 12TH

GLOBAL GRILLED CHEESE

CROQUE MONSIEUR & CROQUE MADAME - *FRANCE*
The Croque Monsieur is what you could consider the "grilled cheese" of France. Often made with a few slices of ham, Gruyère is the most popular choice of cheese for this sandwich.

BOMBAY MASALA CHEESE TOAST SANDWICH - *INDIA*
In India a popular street food choice is the Bombay Masala Cheese sandwich. Typically this sandwich contains a mix of cheese, chutney sauce, vegetables, and Masala spices.

CUBAN - *CUBA*
Prepared on a special type of Cuban bread, this sandwich traditionally uses Swiss cheese and features one or more cuts of pork, pickles, and mustard.

CHEESE AREPA - *SOUTH AMERICA*
Think of this sandwich as a thick corn tortilla filled with cheese. Typically arepas are cooked on a flat top griddle, or in a cast iron pan.

VEGEMITE GRILLED CHEESE - *AUSTRALIA*
Vegemite is a salty yeast based spread that has a savory, concentrated umami flavor. Usually it's spread on toast, but eventually cheese made it onto the sandwich and the Australian grilled cheese was born.

QUESADILLA - *MEXICO*
By now most people know about the quesadilla; a tortilla stuffed with cheese and grilled to toasty perfection. This sandwich is often filled with different types of meat and paired with sour cream or guacamole.

bingin' delicious

BRIE, BING CHERRIES, DUCK FAT, & ARUGULA

W e couldn't figure out if this sandwich was lunch or dessert, but we have confirmed one thing: it's delicious. Flavors inspired by a popular salad have made their way between two slices of bread and onto your dinner table for a knockout combination. This sandwich has been known to cause euphoria, so be weary of operating heavy machinery after consuming one.

2 Tbsp. duck fat

¼ cup pitted cherries, sliced

4 oz. brie cheese (Le Delice Mon Sire brand preferred*) sliced into strips

Small handful arugula

2 slices wheat bread

Method:

Preheat your tools and grill according to the cooking methods on page 10-11. Slice cherries and remove pits. Chop cherries into small pieces and set aside. Spread the top side of each slice of bread with half the duck fat. Take one slice in your hand (fat side down) and add all the sliced cheese. Place cherries and arugula onto the cheese and top with the other slice of bread. Transfer to the grill and cook 3-5 minutes per side until bread is toasted and cheese has melted.

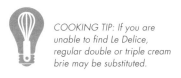

COOKING TIP: If you are unable to find Le Delice, regular double or triple cream brie may be substituted.

after school snack

SHARP CHEDDAR WITH APPLESAUCE

*T*his sandwich is a tribute to those of you still young at heart. Apples on cheddar are a popular snack for the little ones, so naturally the next step is to combine the two with some other kid's favorites: the grilled cheese and apple sauce. Eat them separately or be brave and take a dip! You'll be pleasantly surprised by this intriguing duo of savory and sweet.

Method:

Sandwich:

¼ cup extra sharp cheddar, shredded

2 slices white bread

2 tsp. quality butter

Applesauce:

1 Fuji apple

1 cup apple cider

½ tsp. cinnamon

Remove core from apple and dice into equal-sized small cubes. Places apple into a small sauce pot, add cinnamon, and cover with cider. Simmer on low flame until a fork can pierce the apple with no resistance. Drain apples, reserve liquid and place into a food processor. Purée apples until smooth and pour liquid back in as needed to achieve desired consistency.

Preheat your tools and grill according to the cooking methods on page 10-11.

Remove crust from bread, Take one slice in your hand (butter side down) and add the cheddar and place the other slice of bread on top. Transfer to the grill and cook 4-6 minutes per side until bread is toasted and cheese has melted. Serve alongside apple sauce.

COOKING TIP: Tillamook Extra Sharp Special Reserve is a great cheese to use with this recipe.

sweet b&b

NECTARINES, BRIE & BRIOCHE BREAD

*N*ectarines and Brie make for a fantastic sweet/savory combination appropriate for many applications. Here we've paired them with buttery, rich brioche bread to really ramp up the flavor profile. This summer sandwich recipe can be adjusted to use whichever stone fruit is in season at your local farmers' market.

1 wedge triple cream brie

1 nectarine

2 slices brioche bread

2 tsp. quality butter

Method:

Preheat your tools and grill according to the cooking methods on page 10-11. Cut nectarine in half and remove pit. Slice one half of the nectarine into thin strips. Cut two long strips of brie from the wedge, and cut them into 2 inch sections.

Butter the top side of each slice of bread. Take one slice in your hand (butter side down) and add the brie and 6-7 slices of fruit. Top with the other slice of buttered bread and transfer to the grill. Grill 4-6 minutes per side until bread is toasted and cheese has melted.

BEVERAGE TIP: Serve this grilled cheese alongside a tall glass of iced tea for a tasty, refreshing summer lunch.

sun-dried caprese

PESTO, MOZZARELLA & SUN-DRIED TOMATOES

This sandwich is an intriguing twist on the concept of a classic caprese salad. Basil-infused pesto is spread liberally underneath creamy mozzarella and topped with slow-cooked tangy sun-dried tomatoes. Think of it as a caprese on two giant freshly toasted croutons!

Method:

Preheat a sauté pan over medium flame 20-30 seconds until hot. Add all tomato confit ingredients and cook over low, gentle flame for 8-10 minutes. Remove from pan and cool completely. Preheat your tools and grill according to the cooking methods on page 10-11.

Thinly slice mozzarella and spread pesto on the bottom slice of bread. Layer 3-4 slices of mozzarella on top of the pesto and top with 2 teaspoons of tomato relish. Place the other piece of bread on top and transfer to the preheated grill. Grill 4-6 minutes per side until bread is toasted and cheese has melted.

Sandwich:

1 ball fresh mozzarella cheese (3-4 oz. approx.)

2 tsp. organic pesto

2 slices focaccia bread

Sun-dried Tomato Confit:

¼ cup sun-dried tomatoes, rough chopped

2 small cloves of garlic, minced

½ cup mild flavored olive oil

½ tsp. kosher salt

pinch of fresh oregano

pinch of pepper

BEVERAGE TIP: Try this sandwich with a refreshing Italian pilsner like Peroni.

the parisian

MARSCAPONE & PROSCIUTTO ON A CROISSANT

This sandwich isn't just your average ham 'n cheese. Prepared on a flaky, buttery croissant roll, this combination of creamy mascarpone, prosciutto, and lemon zest is sure to be a hit at your next brunch. Grilling this sandwich gives a smoky background that works well with its flavor profile.

2 Tbsp. mascarpone

1 tsp. parmesan, shredded

2 large slices prosciutto

1 tsp. lemon zest

1 tsp. extra virgin olive oil

1 croissant

Method:

Remove mascarpone from refrigeration 20 minutes before assembling sandwich to soften.

Preheat your tools and grill according to the cooking methods on page 10-11. Slice the croissant in half. Spread the mascarpone on one side, then layer one piece of prosciutto by folding it in an "s" shape on top of itself spanning across half the croissant.

Repeat this with the second piece of prosciutto. Sprinkle lemon zest and parmesan on top of the prosciutto then drizzle with olive oil. Place the other half of the croissant on top. Place the sandwich onto the grill and cook 2-3 minutes per side until just warmed through.

BEVERAGE TIP: Sticking with the citrus and breakfast themes, a mimosa would be the perfect match to enjoy with this sandwich.

nuevo choripán

PEPPERJACK & CHORIZO WITH AVOCADO SOUP

This recipe was designed to take your taste buds on a little trip south of the border. In Argentina, choripán is a simple and very popular street sandwich. Just bread and chorizo, hence the name. So we made a grilled cheese sandwich version using pepperjack cheese combined with a more traditional queso fresco for a nice balance of heat, saltiness, and texture. Just like you would with a nice tomato soup, don't forget to try dipping your sandwich into this refreshing avocado soup, to bring all the flavors of this dish together with one bite.

Method:

Soup:

1 ripe avocado

1 Tbsp. cilantro, minced

1 lime, juiced

water, as needed

Remove pit from avocado and scoop insides out. Place avocado in a food processor with cilantro, lime juice, pinch of salt and pepper and puree. Add water until soup consistency is achieved. Adjust salt and pepper and add additional lime if needed.

Sandwich:

2 tsp. organic mayonnaise

2 slices potato bread

¼ cup pepperjack cheese

2 Tbsp. cooked chorizo

2 Tbsp. queso fresco

Salt, to taste

Pepper, to taste

Preheat your tools and grill according to the cooking methods on page 10-11.

Spread half the mayonnaise on the outside of each slice of bread. Take one slice in your hand (mayo side down) and add the pepperjack, chorizo and queso Fresco. Top with the other slice of mayo-covered bread and transfer to the grill. Grill 4-6 minutes per side until bread is toasted and cheese has melted.

BEVERAGE TIP: This sandwich goes great with a Mexican pilsner style ale such as Sol, Tecate, or Modelo.

panino italiano

MOZZARELLA, PROVOLONE & MUFFULETTA

Inspired by the classic Italian Muffuletta sandwich, this grilled cheese has a refreshingly salty tang from kalamata and picholine olives followed up with the spicy snap of pepperoncini peppers. Combine that with the subtle flavors and rich creaminess of fresh mozzarella and you've got a winning combination. If you're not a meat eater, go ahead and swap the salami for some gently roasted eggplant to make a dynamite vegetarian version!

1 ball fresh mozzarella cheese (3-4 oz. approx.)

1 slice provolone

1 small pepperoncini pepper, seeded and minced

1 tsp. kalamata olives, minced

1 tsp. picholine olives, minced

4 slices Italian dry salami

2 tsp. quality butter

2 slices sourdough bread

Method:

Preheat your tools and grill according to the cooking methods on page 10-11. In a small bowl, combine seeded pepper with olives and mix. Spread top side of each slice of bread with half the butter. Take one slice in your hand (fat side down) and add one slice of provolone with 2-3 slices fresh mozzarella on top.

Add mixed olives and peppers and place buttered second slice of bread on top. Transfer to preheated grill and cook 4-6 minutes per side until bread is crispy and cheese has melted.

COOKING TIP: Serve this sandwich along a hearty vegetable minestrone for a well-rounded Italian inspired dinner.

A special thanks to all The Companion Group® Berkeley office taste testers
for trying so many grilled cheese sandwiches and giving great feedback.

Thanks to all of our contributors:
Chuck Adams, Wendy Boeger, Amaranta Colindres, Niki Gross, & Natalie Torkar

Photography & styling: Sharon Kallenberger & Tiffany Threets
Book design: Tiffany Threets | Recipes: Nick Wellhausen
Copy: Simone Chavoor & Nick Wellhausen